the Book of FaBuLoUs Questions

Great conversation starters about love, sex and other personal stuff

D0806780

the Book of

Fabulous

Questions

**Great conversation starters about
love, sex and other personal stuff**

By *Penelope Frohart*

BRG Publishing
Minneapolis, MN

ISBN 0-9661144-6-9
Library of Congress Catalog Card Number: 98-93474

Manufactured in the United States of America
Fall 1999

Published by:
BRG Publishing
P.O. Box 50693
Minneapolis, MN 55405
brgpublish@aol.com
www.thedatingguru.com

Questions or comments, please call 612-617-7717

10 9 8 7 6 5 4 3 2

Table of Contents

Preface

"How do you know when you're in love?"

Think about that question. How would you answer it? How would your friends answer it? And is it really as simple as it sounds?

Well, in this book there are more than 600 thought provoking questions like it. Some easy, some complicated, some admittedly controversial. Use them as you wish, you'll find they'll spice up any conversation. Questions can be posed to friends, spouses, casual acquaintances, lovers, relatives, just about anyone! They're intended, at the very least, to initiate some fun and perhaps lively conversations. They may even open up conversational territories previously unknown and unexplored.

Every question has the potential for leading almost anywhere. Even the most innocent-seeming question can trigger a unique thought process and turn out being far more revealing than originally intended. And that, of course, is the real purpose of this book.

Some questions may serve as ice-breakers with new acquaintances. Some will help you understand and get to know someone even better. Some will even help you to get a better grasp of yourself. So, no matter how you use this book, we promise you a great time with it.

Most of these questions are intended to get the ball rolling. They may be used in light situations where a smile or a laugh is the intent. Or, they may be casually inserted where more meaningful information is the objective.

The Book of Fabulous Questions can also be used as a game. Games between two people, or several. So, it can be a wonderful party device, good for hours of fascinating responses and discussions. You never know what may be revealed. Your good judgment will tell you how, where and when to use this book. Certain questions will surely motivate you to invent more and add to the list as you go.

These questions have been pre-tested to see how well they work in conversations. We can tell you they work exceedingly well!

We'd love to hear from you! After you've used this book in different situations and circumstances, tell us all about the experience and what kind of responses you received. Send us questions you'd like to see in a sequel or answers that shocked you.
Send to: BRG Publishing, PO Box 50693,
              Minneapolis, MN 55405.

Thank you. Oh, yes, and enjoy!

Stage I:
In All Innocence

Questions of Youth

When were you born? What city were you born in?

What different things did you want to be when you grew up?

What was your most memorable childhood experience? How has it impacted your outlook on life?

Were you a good or a bad kid? Would your parents agree with you?

What were your favorite toys to play with? Do you still have any of them?

What cartoon character did you like the best when you were younger?

Did you have an imaginary friend? How would you describe them?

What do you remember about your first day of school?

What was your neighborhood like when you were younger?

How often did your family move while you were growing up?

What was your favorite
school lunch?

Who was your most
memorable baby-sitter?
What made them so
memorable?

What was your favorite game to play when you were younger?

Did you ever run away from home? Where did you go? How long were you gone?

How often did you host or attend slumber parties?

What were you teased about when you were younger? How did that make you feel? Did you tease others?

Who was your first best friend? How long did the friendship last?

What was your favorite subject in school? What was your least favorite subject? What kind of grades did you get in those subjects?

Did you get an
allowance? How much?
How did you earn it?

What school sports and
activities did you
participate in?

Where was your favorite place to hang out when you were younger? How often did you go there?

How often were you grounded? What caused you to get grounded?

Did you ever sneak out of your family home? Where did you go? Were you caught?

Did you ever hang out with the wrong crowd in school? What was the result?

Have you ever cheated on a test? How? Did you feel guilty? Were you caught?

How often were you sent to the Principal's office? Were you ever suspended?

What do you remember about the first dance you attended?

What kind of car did you use to learn how to drive?

What was your first job? How much were you paid?

What were your goals when you graduated from high school? Did you succeed at reaching them?

What did you like best about high school? What did you like least about high school?

At what age did you hit puberty? What changes did you notice? Were you an early or late bloomer?

What's your memory of prom (date, place, attire)?

Who were your high school sweethearts? Have you kept in touch with any of them?

Questions
of Family

Have you ever traced
your ancestry? What
did you find out?

What nationality are
you? Do you know
much about the culture?

Have you had an opportunity to get to know your grandparents? What's your greatest memory of them?

Do you like your name? If you could change it, what would you change it to?

Which of your qualities do you attribute to your mom? Which of your qualities do you attribute to your dad? Which qualities are uniquely your own?

How would your parents describe what it was like to raise you as a child? What would they say their most frustrating memory of raising you was?

29

How would your mom describe you? How would you describe your mom?

How would your dad describe you? How would you describe your dad?

Are you more similar to your mom or your dad?

How would you describe the members of your family?

What makes the difference between a good parent and a great parent?

Do you consider your parents equal?

What's the biggest fight you've had with your family?

How often do you see your family? Do you think that's enough?

What was your most
memorable family
vehicle?

Did you have a family
pet when you were
growing up?

Which family member
are you closest to?

If you could change one
thing about your family,
what would it be?

How would you describe the perfect family reunion (when. where. who)?

Does your family have a nickname for you?

How would your parents describe the perfect mate for you? Do you agree with their description?

Do you keep any secrets from your family?

What TV family would you compare your family to?

What was your worst family vacation? **W**hy was it so bad?

What was your best family vacation? What made it so great?

How did your parents discipline you? Would you discipline your children the same way? Why?

What's your family
most proud of you for?

When's the right time to
start a family of your
own?

What would your ideal
family consist of?

Do you want your
children to grow up just
like you? Why?

What family traditions
will you carry on into
your own family?

If your children could
remember only one lesson
in life, what would you
teach them? How would
you teach it to them?

42

Would you choose the sex of your unborn child if you could? Which sex would you choose? Why?

Do you already have names in mind for your future children?

Questions of Friendship

Who is your best friend? What makes them special?

How would your best friend describe you?

Do your closest friends tend to be men or women? Why do you think this is?

What's most common among all of your friends?

What do you and your
friends usually do for
fun?

How would you
describe your closest
friends? Are they similar
to you or opposite?

How would your closest
friends describe you?

How often do friends
come to you for advice?
How often do you seek
advice from them?

How would your friends describe the way you act when you're angry?

How would your friends describe the way you act when you're happy?

If friends from high school were to see you now, what would they think?

Name one thing you wouldn't want your friends to know about you? How would they react if they found out?

When was the last time you fought with a friend? What was the fight about? How did you resolve it?

Do you make new friends easily?

How did you meet the majority of your current friends?

Define a good friend? Do you consider yourself a good friend?

Which of your friends have you known the longest?

Are most of your friends single or attached?

What's the nicest thing
a friend has done for you?
What's the nicest thing
you've done for a friend?

How do you distinguish
between a friend and an
acquaintance?

Which of your friends
are you the most similar
to?

Which of your friends
are you opposite of?

Questions
of Career

What are your parent's
occupations?

How did you end up in
your current job?

Did you go to college?
Where? For how long?

What was your major
in college? How did you
choose it?

Do you think a college degree is necessary to get a job?

How valuable has your education been?

What do you love and hate the most about your current job? Do you love more things than you hate?

What are your greatest strengths and weaknesses as an employee? What have you done to improve your weaknesses?

58

Are you paid what
you're worth? What do
you base your worth on?

What's the greatest
career challenge you've
faced? How did you
handle it?

How do you foresee
your career situation five
years from now?

What were the two
most significant turning
points in your career?
How did they change
your life?

What are your career
goals? How do you plan
to achieve them?

Is your current position
where you thought you'd
be five years ago?

How would your boss
describe you? How
would you describe your
boss?

Would you make a good
boss? Why?

How would you
describe your ideal boss?

Do you prefer your
superiors to be the same
sex as you or the opposite
sex? Why?

Would you sleep your way to the top?

What are your views on affirmative action?

64

What's your ideal job?

Do you work better individually or with a team? Why do you think that is?

Have you ever been in a work situation where you had to sacrifice your own morals or ethics? How did you handle it?

How many times have you called in sick and not really been sick?

Have you ever embarrassed yourself at a work social function?

Have you ever dated someone you worked with? How did it work out?

Have you ever asked for a raise? Did you get it?

Have you ever been passed up for a promotion? How did that make you feel?

Do you work well
under pressure?

What's the toughest
work related decision
you've had to make?
What was the outcome?

Who do you use as references? If I called them, what would they say about you?

What makes your job worth getting up for?

Are you confident with your interviewing skills? What's your strongest selling point?

Do you feel you make a difference with your job?

What preparation would you need to step into your boss's shoes?

Who do you model yourself after professionally? What about them do you admire?

Do you consider yourself a hard-worker? Based on what?

On average, how many hours do you work in a given week?

Does your job make you feel proud?

In your life priorities, where does your career fall?

Stage II: Mild Curiosity

Questions of Personal Experiences

Who would you prefer
to never speak to again?
What made them so
undesirable?

What event in your life
would you like to
permanently forget?

What's the most regrettable thing you've ever done to someone? How do you think their life was changed as a result?

What's your most embarrassing moment?

77

What's the dumbest
argument you've had?
Who started it?

What's the biggest party
you've ever thrown or
attended?

What's the nicest thing a stranger has ever done for you? How did it make you feel?

What's the nicest thing you've ever done for a stranger? Why did you do it?

When's the last time you sent or received flowers?

What have you been caught doing that you regret? Do you regret doing it or just getting caught?

What's the greatest personal challenge you've ever faced? How did it change you?

What have you always wanted to do, but haven't? Why haven't you done it?

81

What was the last movie you saw in a theater? What was the last movie you rented?

How would you describe your most memorable birthday?

Have you ever experienced road rage? What happened?

Have you ever been physically or mentally abused? How did you handle it?

Do you consider yourself a revengeful person? Who have you tried to get even with? Why?

Have you ever answered or placed a personal ad? What was the result?

84

When was the last time
you gave a speech? What
was it about?

Have you ever been in a
physical fight? Who
started it? What was the
outcome?

What has made you mad beyond belief? How did you handle the situation? Did it change your attitude about anything?

What's the worst dream you've ever had? What's your interpretation?

What one quality do you possess that makes you feel special when someone recognizes it?

What has been your favorite daydream in recent years?

What's the biggest lie you've ever told? Did anyone find out?

What's the biggest prank you've played on someone? What's the biggest prank ever played on you?

What's your greatest
personal strength?   How
has it helped you in life?

What personal quality
would you like to
improve the most?

When have you felt the most proud of yourself? When have you felt the most disappointed in yourself?

Have you ever stolen anything? Why? Were you caught?

What lessons have you learned the hard way? Do you tend to learn from your mistakes the first time or after a couple of times?

Who has had the greatest positive impact on your life?

91

Have you ever had a mentor? What did you learn from them?

What situations have you been able to talk your way out of?

Have you ever mooned someone? Have you ever been mooned?

Have you ever had a near death experience? What was it like? How did it make you feel?

Have you ever lost
someone very close to
you? What effect did it
have on you?

Think back five years
ago, how did you think
your life would be today?
How's it different from
what you pictured?

Which of your personal beliefs do you feel so strongly about that you will never compromise?

Have you ever spied on someone? What did you discover?

What was your best
Halloween costume ever?

When was the last time
you really went out of
your way for someone?
What did you do? Why?

Have you ever been arrested?

What has been your experience with drugs?

What's one mistake no one will let you forget?

What's the stupidest thing you've ever done while you were drunk?

What has been your
scariest experience?

How do you pamper
yourself?

How often do you dress up?

Who do you turn to when you are sad, lonely, angry or upset?

Name one thing that
you are constantly
putting off? Why?

Are you spontaneous?
What's the most
spontaneous thing you've
ever done?

How well do you keep secrets?

Has anyone ever said that you look like a celebrity? Who?

How often do you take risks?

What's your idea of roughing it? How often do you go camping?

What's the craziest
thing you've ever done on
a dare?

When's the last time
you cried? Why?

Who makes you feel inferior?

Have you ever attended a high school or college reunion? What was it like?

What's your greatest insecurity?

Have you ever been hospitalized?

Who's the most famous person you've met?

What's your greatest fear?

What was the first
concert you attended?

Do you collect
anything?

Do you prefer to be the passenger or the driver? Are you a back seat driver?

Do you have a tattoo? If you got one, what would you get and where?

Have you ever hitch-hiked?

How do you celebrate good news?

Are you stubborn?
Give an example?

What experience has
given you an extreme
adrenaline rush?

Questions of Favorites

What are your favorite
leisure activities?

What's your favorite
holiday? Why?

What's your favorite
fruit?

What's your favorite
vegetable?

What's your favorite season? Why?

What's your favorite movie of all-time?

What's your favorite song? How does it make you feel?

What's your favorite animal?

What's your favorite fast food joint? How often do you eat there?

What's your favorite alcoholic beverage?

What's your favorite ice cream flavor?

What's your favorite candy bar?

What are your favorite
kind of potato chips?

What's your favorite
dessert?

What's your favorite color?

What's your favorite restaurant?

What's your favorite
breakfast food?

What's your favorite
radio station? What
kind of music do you
listen to?

What's your favorite outfit? How does it make you feel?

Where's your favorite place to relax?

What's your favorite
TV show?

What's your favorite
food?

What's your favorite
sport?

Where's your favorite
place to travel?

Where's your favorite
place to be alone?

What's your favorite
perfume or cologne?

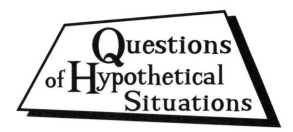

Questions of Hypothetical Situations

If you could travel back in time, and change how you handled one event in your life, what would you change?

If you could send a letter that traveled back through time, what would you write to yourself?

If you could travel into
the future, where would
you go? How would you
use the knowledge when
you came back to the
present?

If you could travel back
in time, where would
you go? What would
you like to experience?

If you could have a dinner party with any three people in the world, who would you invite?

If you could spend one night with the person of your dreams, would you do it even if meant risking a current relationship?

If you were to write a
personal ad, what would
it say?

If you could be
transformed into any
animal for one day, which
animal would you select?
What kind of experience
would you expect?

If you could be the best at
anything in the world,
what would you choose?
Why?

If you were granted the
true answer to any one
question in the universe,
what would you ask?
What would you do
with this knowledge?

If you were condemned to eat only one ethnic food for the rest of your life, which would you choose?

If you could change one of your personality characteristics, what would you change? How do you think your life would be different?

If you could change one
of your physical features,
what would you change?
How do you think your
life would be different?

If you were to become a
mentor, who would you
like to help and what
kind of wisdom would
you offer them?

131

If the world was going to
end in 15 minutes, what
would be your last words
to me?

If you won a billion
dollar lottery, what
would you do with the
money?

If you won an all expense paid trip for two weeks, where would you go?

If you were to give me words of wisdom from your experiences, what would you say?

If you were to cook a romantic dinner, what would the menu consist of?

If I looked in your top drawer, what would I find?

If you could do something totally out of character and remain anonymous, what would you do?

If your life could be described by the title of a song, what would the title be?

If a genie granted you three wishes. what would you wish for? Would you try to talk the genie into giving you an extra wish?

If your personality was characterized by the weather. what would your forecast be?

If I looked in your refrigerator right now, what would I see?

If someone has food in their teeth or their zipper is down, will you tell them? Does it make a difference whether you know them or not?

137

If you had magical
powers to do anything,
how would you use
them?

If you were the only one
to find out that the world
would end in exactly one
week, would you tell
everyone to prepare them
or keep the information
to yourself?

If you could choose the cause of your death, what would you choose?

If you could be someone else for the next 24 hours, who would you want to be? Why? What would you do?

If you could live your life
in a movie, what movie
and character would you
pick? Why?

If everyone was exactly
like you, what would the
world be like?

If you could build a vacation home anywhere in the world, where would you build it?

If you could be famous for one thing, what would it be?

If you could write the
eulogy for your funeral,
what would it say?
Who would read it?

If you hit a car and did
significant damage, but
no one saw it, would you
leave a note or just leave?

If you were offered two million dollars to leave your country and not contact anyone again, would you take it and start over?

If you could live one year of your life all over again without changing a thing, what year would you choose? Why?

If you could live one day of your life all over again without changing a thing, what day would you choose? Why?

If you were stranded on a desert island and could only have two things with you, what would they be?

If I looked in your wallet right now, what would I find?

If you could be a cartoon character, which character would you choose?

If your wardrobe could only be one color, which color would you choose?

If you could only live in one season all year 'round, which season would you choose?

Stage III: In Your Face

Questions of Dating

How can you tell if someone is interested in you? How do you show interest in someone?

What's the most creative way you've been approached by someone interested in you?

What's the most creative way you've introduced yourself to someone?

How do you prefer to be approached by someone interested in you?

What's the best pick-up line you've heard or used? Did it work?

Based on your experience, where's the best place to meet potential dates?

What do you think potential dates find most appealing about you?

What types of people tend to be attracted to you?

What has been your best experience with a blind date? Did it lead to another date?

What has been your worst experience with a blind date? How did it end?

How would you describe your ideal first date? At what point do you decide if there will be a second?

What's your idea of a romantic date? How many dates have you been on like that?

Have you ever dated someone who was married? If not, would you consider it?

Have you ever dated someone your friends or family disliked? If not, would you?

Do you believe opposites
attract? Can opposites be
compatible?

Do you tend to date
people similar to you or
opposite of you?

Describe the most opposite person you've dated? What attracted you to them?

Describe the most similar person you've dated? What attracted you to them?

Do you always kiss on a first date?

How do you feel about having sex on a first date?

Do you tend to date
people older or younger
than you? Why?

Among everyone you've
dated, what characteristics
seem to be the most
common?

How do you feel about public displays of affection? Where do you draw the line?

What have your mother and father warned you about dating? Do you take their advice?

What's the worst date you've ever had? What's the best date you've ever had? How did they end?

How have you met most of the people you've dated?

What's the most
unusual circumstance in
which you've met
someone you dated?

What's your time frame
for when dating turns
into a relationship?

How long does it usually take you to know whether the person you are dating has what it takes for a relationship? Do you test them?

What standards do you set for dating? Do you make any exceptions?

Do you tend to date people with similar characteristics (tall, dark hair, blue eyes)?

How often do you exchange phone numbers with people you meet? Once you get a phone number, how long do you wait to call? How soon do you expect to be called?

What's the most annoying thing someone could do on a first date? What would be the result?

Who have you dated far longer than you should have? Why did you wait so long to end it?

Do you think men and women can be just friends?

Do you consider yourself a flirt? How do you flirt?

Do you often date more than one person at a time?

What's the most number of people you've dated at one time? How did it work out?

Questions of Relationships

What did your previous
mate do that really
turned you off?

What's the worst break-
up you've experienced?
Why was is so bad?

What's the easiest break-up you've experienced? Why was it so easy?

How do you break up with someone? Do you tell them face-to-face? Do you break it off in public or private?

Under what circumstances are you able to remain friends with an ex? Under what circumstances are you not able to remain friends with an ex?

How many of your friends have you dated in the past?

What's the worst thing an ex could say about you? What's the worst thing you could say about an ex?

What's the best thing an ex could say about you? What's the best thing you could say about an ex?

What has been your biggest let-down in a relationship? What was the result?

Would you continue a relationship with someone who cheated on you?

Have you ever been cheated on? What impact did it have on you?

Have you ever cheated on someone? Why? Did you feel guilty? Did they find out?

Do you find it difficult to be faithful in a relationship?

If your mate was sharing sexual fantasies on-line, would you consider it cheating?

173

What's the single most important thing in a relationship? Why is it so important to you?

How do you approach issues in a relationship?

What's the most romantic gift you've ever received? What was the occasion?

What's the least romantic gift you've ever received? How did you react?

What's the most romantic and least romantic gift you've ever given someone?

Have you ever lived with your mate? If not, would you? If so, what was it like?

Are you a jealous
person? What makes
you jealous in a
relationship?

At what stage do you
introduce your mate to
your parents?

Do you consider monogamy a must in a relationship? Do you discuss it first or is it just expected?

How do you decide when you want an exclusive relationship with someone?

What's the longest relationship you've ever been in? Do you regret it?

What's the best asset you bring into a relationship? Would others agree?

179

In your relationship priorities, where does sex rate?

Do you ever play hard to get? Under what circumstances?

180

Have you ever snooped through your mate's drawers? What were you looking for? What did you find?

Do you keep pictures of your past lovers?

Have you ever been stalked by an ex or anyone else?

Who do you regret being in a relationship with? What did you learn from it?

What's your mate's
biggest complaint about
you?

What would you most
like to know about your
mate, if you could find out
without them knowing?

What was your first impression upon meeting your mate? Has that impression changed?

What one quality in your mate do you appreciate the most?

Does your mate annoy you without realizing it? How do you bring it to their attention?

Name one thing your mate could do that would automatically end the relationship?

How do you feel when your mate talks about past relationships?

Does your mate do anything that embarrasses you?

How do you feel if your mate makes more money than you?

Do you consistently communicate your feelings to your mate?

How long did you know
your current mate before
you dated?

Which of your mate's
friends do you find
attractive?

What would make you lose respect for your mate?

On a scale of 1-1 0 how well do you know your mate?

Questions of Love

Do you feel you understand love? What is your definition of love?

Is it easier for you to fall in or out of love?

190

How do you know
when you're in love?

How do you tell
someone you love them
for the first time?

Who was your first love? How old were you? What became of it?

What's the biggest sacrifice you've made for love?

What was it about your previous mate that made you fall in love?

Who have you had the most difficulty getting over? Why?

How many people have
you said "I Love You" to?

Can you identify couples
that are in love?

Do you feel different when you're in love?

How many different types of love do you think there are? How would you describe the differences?

What's your favorite
love song?

How many hearts have
you broken?

How many times has your heart been broken?

How many times have you fallen so deeply in love that you felt it would last forever?

What's the most romantic thing you've done for someone special?

What five words describe your perfect mate? Why are they so important? Do most people you date have these traits? How has your idea of a perfect mate evolved over the past 5 years?

What's the secret behind couples who have been happily married for over 30 years?

How often do you write love letters? Do you save past love letters?

After a quarrel, are you the first to kiss and make up or is your mate?

What's the best thing about being in love?

Do you feel love is necessary for a relationship to progress?

Does love make you do strange things?

Do you fear
commitment?

Have you ever been
engaged?

Would you sign a prenuptial agreement? Why?

Before you got married, would you live with your future spouse to test it out? What if it was a bad experience?

How would you describe your dream wedding?

How would you describe your ideal honeymoon?

Stage IV: None Of Your Business

Questions of Habits

How many times a day
do you brush your teeth?

Do you snore?

What are your sleeping habits (blanket hog, sleep in the middle of the bed)?

Do you keep a diary? Whose diary would you most want to read? Why?

Do you sing in the shower?

Are you a punctual person or are you usually late?

Do you like to cuddle while you sleep or roll over to your own side?

Do you plan ahead or take one day at a time?

How often do you cook?
How often do you eat
out?

Do you obey all traffic
laws?

How many hours a week do you spend watching TV?

What style of underwear do you wear?

Do you consider yourself in shape? How often do you exercise per week?

How often do you read the newspaper or watch the news?

How frequently do you strike up conversations with strangers?

How often do you read? What's the last book you read?

How often do you get sick?

What do you wear to sleep in?

Do you screen phone calls before answering the phone?

How long does it take you to get ready in the morning?

In heated arguments do you walk away or keep at it until you've had the final word?

How many times a day do you look in a mirror? Can you walk past one without looking?

What's your worst
habit? How did it start?
Can you stop it?

Do you tend to focus
more on the past, present
or future?

Do you shy away from cameras or welcome them?

How often do you balance your checkbook?

How well do you
remember important
dates, such as birthdays?

What's the first thing
you do when you wake
up?

What five words would you use to describe yourself? Can you give an example of how you possess each characteristic?

Do you tend to blame others for your problems?

How much of life depends on luck? Do you consider yourself lucky?

What was your first impression of me? How has it evolved?

What's the greatest difference between us? What's the greatest similarity?

Do you fear death?

Do you consider yourself spiritual? How do you define spirituality?

What are your religious beliefs? Do your religious beliefs influence your everyday decisions?

How often do you pray?
Why do you pray?

What are your top three
pet peeves?

How often do you travel? Do you travel mostly for business or pleasure?

Will our country be better or worse in five years? What makes you feel that way?

Do you think men have
it easier than women?
When is it harder to be a
man? When is it harder
to be a woman?

Is compromise hard for
you? Why?

Where is your most ticklish spot?

What are you allergic to?

What famous quotation do you live by?

Do you consider yourself athletic? What sports do you like to play?

What talents do you
have that would surprise
me?

What's your sign? How
often do you read your
horoscope? Do you
believe in it?

Do you like to dance?
What's your best dance
move?

On average, how many
alcoholic drinks do you
consume in a week?

Who's your idol? Do you model yourself after them?

What could someone do for you that would make you very happy?

How can someone tell if you're happy? How can someone tell if you're sad?

Do you consider yourself an organized person? Why?

Who makes you laugh
the most?

Would you ever go to an
all-nude beach?

What does your driving
record look like?

How would you
describe your driving
style (cautious, reckless,
fast, slow)?

Do you classify yourself
as a leader or a follower?

What character in the
Wizard of Oz are you
most like? Why?

Approximately, how many pairs of shoes do you own?

How often do you shop for new clothes?

How gullible are you?

Do you like amusement parks? When's the last time you were on a roller coaster?

What do you constantly worry about?

How have you changed the most since you were younger?

What's the last joke you heard?

How do you feel about people who gossip? Do you join in or ignore them?

Does your personality match your physical appearance?

Do you act your age?

Are you the type of person who openly shares their opinion or do you wait until you're asked your opinion?

What do you do in support of the environment?

Is it better to give or to receive? Honestly?

Would you give me your car keys without hesitation?

What's one thing you can't say NO to?

What do you think is the greatest invention of our time?

How often do you
watch sports?

How are you prepared
to protect yourself in a
threatening situation?

How often do you compliment people? Do you receive more compliments than you give?

Name one thing you will not leave home without?

How good is your sense of direction? Do you stop and ask for directions when you are lost?

Which of the Seven Dwarfs are you the most similar to?

Are you a good listener?

It's said that people are what they eat. what are you?

Are you superstitious?
To what extent?

Do you believe in ghosts
or extraterrestrial
beings?

How many hours of sleep do you need per night to be fully functional in the morning?

Do you embarrass easily?

Do you tend to
exaggerate things?

Are you planning to
donate your organs when
you die?

How patient are you?
Give an example?

How competitive are
you? Give an example?

How well do you know your neighbors?

What are your hobbies?

Are you a morning or night person?

What brings out the child in you?

What brings out the animal in you?

How do you relax?

Describe your ideal vacation?

Do you consider yourself financially stable?

How do you act when you're angry?

Do you speak any foreign languages fluently?

Are you pro-choice or pro-life?

Do you regularly set goals for yourself? Do you set goals that challenge you or ones that you know you can achieve?

What's your biggest fear?

What effect does stress have on you? How do you deal with it?

Do you enjoy quiet time
to yourself? How often?

What motivates you?

What setting are you the most comfortable in?

What expectations do you have of the people in your life?

When are you totally at peace?

Do you enjoy your own company?

Do you ask for help or support when you need it?

Do you vote regularly?

What's your opinion of our president?

Are you liberal or conservative?

How involved are you in politics?

What's your position on capital punishment?

How would you describe your ultimate dream house?

Do you believe people can change?

Who would you die for?

Do you prefer to live
alone or with someone?

When's the last time you went skinny-dipping?

What musical instruments do you play?

Are you mechanically
inclined?

Have you ever traveled
out of the country?

Do you have a passport?

Do you set limits for yourself when you drink? Do you cut yourself off? How do you know when you've had enough?

Who knows you better than anyone?

What's the most unattractive body part of the opposite sex? **W**hy?

How do you define happiness?

On average, how much is your long distance phone bill?

Questions of Sex

When's the last time you had very satisfying sex? How do you define satisfying sex?

Judging from a scale of 1-10, how dirty is your mind?

What do you wish your lover would do more of in bed?

Do you want your lover to tell you when you haven't sexually satisfied them?

Would you dump someone if you realized they were terrible in bed?

When was your last vivid erotic dream?

Have you been photographed or videotaped naked?

How many times a day do you think about sex?

Have you ever had sex with two or more different people within a 24 hour period?

Do you hide fantasies from your lover that might upset them?

What are your fetishes?

Judging from a scale of 1-10, how strong is your sex drive?

Do you compare your lover to past lovers?

What method of birth control do you prefer?

Have you been tested for HIV or an STD? What was the result?

How would you react if your lover tested positive for an STD?

Do you always discuss birth control with a lover before you have sex?

Do you get into role playing (doctor/nurse, milkman, French maid)?

What props have you used during sex (ice, food, whip cream, toys)?

What's your most embarrassing moment during sex?

Does size matter? Have you compared yourself to others?

Do you discuss sex with your friends? What kind of things do you share with each other?

How would you describe the most memorable sex you've ever had?

Have you ever faked an orgasm?

Have you ever had sex in a public area?

How do you feel about anal sex?

How would your lover react if you shared a desire for a unique sexual experience?

What's your favorite fantasy?

Who have you
fantasized about having
sex with?

What places do you
fantasize about having
sex at?

What fantasy of yours
embarrasses you?

When you first meet
someone, do you wonder
what they're like in bed?

What's the most times you've had sex within a 24 hour period?

What makes you feel sexy?

Do you think you're
sexy when you're naked?

What makes you lust
after someone (looks,
personality, style)?

What body part of the opposite sex turns you on the most?

Who did you fantasize about when you were a teen?

Do you ever fantasize about someone other than your partner during sex?

How would you react if your lover wanted to try a sexual act you considered distasteful?

Where are the most adventurous places you've had sex?

Is your sex style passive or aggressive?

Are you silent or noisy during sex?

How do you handle it when you or your lover isn't in the mood?

293

How do you define intimacy?

Who taught you about the "Birds & the Bees"? How old were you?

Do you prefer to make the first move or have it be made on you?

When's the last time you were blindfolded? What happened during this time?

Do you enjoy being restrained? With what devices?

What's the biggest turn on for you?

What's your most
sensitive body part?

How do you
communicate your sexual
wants and needs with
your lover?

What part of your
lover's past bothers you
the most?

What percentage of
people do you think are
virgins?

Was losing your virginity memorable? Where did it take place? How old were you?

What's the longest you've waited to have sex in a relationship?

Have you ever been or gotten someone pregnant?

Is there a difference between sex and making love? What?

What's the difference
between a good lover and
a great lover?

What's your favorite
position? Will you
consider new positions or
do you stay with what's
familiar?

Do you have a preference between sex in the morning or at night?

Do you talk dirty during sex?

Judging from a scale of 1-10, how experienced are you sexually?

Have you ever had phone sex? Under what circumstances?

Do you have any
cravings after sex?

Do you prefer the lights
on or off during sex?

When was the last time you were in a "sex store"?

Have you ever watched a porno?

What are your secret desires?

Have you had sex in your parent's house? Did you feel guilty?

Have you ever been caught or watched in the act? By who?

Have you ever had a one night stand? Do you regret it?

Have you ever been involved in a threesome? If not, would you? Under what circumstances?

If your lover became your "slave for a day" what would you make them do?

What's your ideal
number of times to have
sex per week?

Do you like to cuddle
after sex?

How often do you masturbate? What triggers it?

What works as an aphrodisiac for you?

What scents turn you on?

What do you think about during sex?

Which two of your five senses do you concentrate on the most during sex?

Could you give up sex for one year if it was for a good cause?

What's the longest you've gone without sex?

What sexual activity do you find absolutely repulsive? Is everything else fair game?

How many people have you slept with? Have you ever lied to anyone about that number? How would your mate react if they knew how many people you've really slept with?

Does a person's sexual history matter if they are already committed to you?

Could you recognize
your lover in the dark?
How?

Have you ever had a
sexual arrangement with
a friend?

How do you set the mood?

What song makes you think about sex?

Do prefer your lovers to be experienced or innocent?

On average, how long do your sexual encounters usually last from beginning to end?

How important is foreplay to you? What do you consider foreplay? How long does it last?

What's the most sensual thing someone could do to you?

ORDER FORM

Please send me the following books:

___ *The Fabulous Book of Questions:* Great
conversation starters about love, sex and other
personal stuff ($9.95)

___ *I Love You:* How to Say I Love You in 99 Different
Languages ($12.95)

✉ Mail Orders: BRG Publishing, P.O. Box 50693,
Minneapolis, MN 55405

Name: _____

Address: _____

City:_____ State:_____ Zip: _____

Phone: (_____) _____

Number of books: _____

Shipping: $3.00 per book

Payment Total: _____

❏ Check   ❏ Money Order

Don't Delay, Order Today!

About the Author

Penelope Frohart is a vibrant young woman with an intense curiosity about people. Over time, she has developed a passion for writing, and this book has come about out of a habit of writing down every conceivable question one human being could ask another. When the list totaled as many as 600, she had the basis for a unique book. We thought so, too.

And because this is a book of questions, we sat down with Frohart and fired away with a few questions of our own.

Q: O.K. Penelope, you want to know so much. How about telling us something about yourself? For example, where are you from? A: I was born in Iowa, but I've lived in Oregon and Michigan and currently reside in Minnesota.

Q: What was your major in college? A: I originally went to school for physical therapy, but after nearly failing my biology class I decided to stay away from anything involving science, especially plant and frog reproduction. After wandering through many subjects, I discovered my true love is writing! This led to a degree in advertising and public relations with an emphasis in marketing and journalism from Grand Valley State University in Grand Rapids, Michigan.

Q: What's your most embarrassing moment? A: I was at a water park and went down this huge slide and landed awkwardly under a surge of water. When I came up, gasping for air and getting my hair out of my face, I noticed everyone staring at me because my bikini top was not where it should've been. To top that off, my friend's grandfather said "Hey, can you do that again?" Needless to say, that was my last trip down the slide that day.

Well, that gives you a little taste of the Frohart persona. In a bit more serious vein, we can tell you that Penelope's been writing all her life. She's produced a number of articles and turned out hundreds of press releases. Her perpetual confidence tells her that "The Book of Fabulous Questions" will be an instant hit. So here it is, and there's another book on the way.